Opening Doors

Making Sense of Life and Death

Wilma Taylor Jones

Michael Moore

VANTAGE PRESS
New York

Illustrated by Rosanne Kaloustian

FIRST EDITION

Published by Vantage Press, Inc.
516 West 34th Street, New York, New York 10001

Manufactured in the United States of America
ISBN: 0-533-12813-7

Library of Congress Catalog Card No.: 98-90483

0 9 8 7 6 5 4 3 2 1

To my grandchildren:
Michael Dean Moore,
Evan Nicole, Aaron Thomas,
and Griffin Hazen Plew

Preface

When I was three years old a one-year-old brother died. I went to the funeral and was disturbed seeing dirt put over his casket. I said nothing to anyone. My father died when I was five years old. I didn't want to go to the funeral. My mother wisely let me attend school instead, although she didn't know it was because I didn't want to see Daddy covered with dirt. I never expressed my feelings, nor was I asked to. I had many questions that remained unanswered until I was an adult.

That is the reason I wrote this book. I know children often can't express their feelings and questions. Michael did and my hope is that his questions will help less vocal children express theirs and give them answers or, at least, open up discussions between children and adults.

Acknowledgments

I would like to acknowledge with special thanks the Rev. George Warren, who encouraged me to write down Michael's theological journey toward truth, and Michael, who gave me permission to write his story and for his critique of it.

I also want to recognize and thank Susan Adams, Harriet Bevil, Maggie Casto, and my sister, Frances Louise Taylor, who read early drafts and offered suggestions, and my husband, Frank Jones, Jr., who patiently supported my vision for this book.

The photograph on the back of this book was taken by Joseph Lowery of Tulsa, Oklahoma.

Opening Doors

Michael is a little boy who likes to play ball, draw pictures, work puzzles, build with Legos, and read books. He has asked God, "Do you put ideas into writers' heads for books or do they think of it themselves?" He has red hair and everyone seems to have something to say about it, such as: "What nice red hair"; "Where did you get your red hair?"; and so forth. Sometimes the attention makes him feel embarrassed. He was born on Sunday and he has attended church almost every Sunday since. When he was three years old he told his grandparents all he wanted for Christmas was a nativity set. They asked him why he wanted that? "Because, *that* is Christmas!" he answered.

Michael's father and mother are employed as accountants. When he was a baby, his mother's parents took care of him in their home while his own parents worked. When he became old enough to walk and talk, his parents took him to La Petite Day Care each day to stay. When he was five years old, he graduated and started to attend public school kindergarten and stayed at a church day care center after school was out.

Michael's father's parents and mother's parents all live in the same city that he lives in, so he sees them often. He calls his mother's parents Ma and Pa. He calls his father's parents Granny and Granny-Pa.

Ma and Pa live in a house with a large backyard that Michael can play ball in. They have a dachshund dog named Lys Star and a gray-and-white cat named Plain Jane.

Ma likes to work in her iris garden and read books. She had a stroke and has to wear a brace on her lower left leg and ankle. The brace is fastened to her shoe. She also uses a cane to help her walk. Michael sometimes pretends that her cane is a microphone or a horse. Ma reads to him until he goes to sleep for a nap, but, he knows she will go to sleep first. What do you suppose he does? He waits until she goes to sleep, then he slips off the bed and starts playing. He tells Pa that he put Ma to sleep.

Pa collects stamps and he likes to work puzzles and watch ballgames on TV. He mostly likes the Arkansas Razorbacks because he went to school at the University of Arkansas.

Michael had a favorite stuffed bunny that he got for Easter when he was one month old. When he was sad, scared, or hurt someplace, he felt better when he chewed or rubbed Bunny's long ears. He took Bunny with him every place he went. At Ma and Pa's house, he also had a quilt, made by a friend, and a stuffed Snoopy dog with big ears to sleep with.

Granny and Granny-Pa had a model windmill in their front yard. They had both grown up on farms in Arkansas. Granny liked to cook. She had worked in a cafeteria at one time.

Michael enjoyed going to Granny and Granny-Pa's for Easter, Thanksgiving, and Christmas when his father's sisters and brother and their families all came. Granny always made chicken and dumplings. They had a big meal and lots of visiting and playing with cousins. All their family and friends came to a big party to celebrate their fiftieth Wedding Anniversary.

When Michael was two years old, his parents divorced. He now lives with his mother and her gray cat named Fergus in a house with a large yard. Michael's father lives in an apartment in the same city. He visits his father every other weekend and lives with him for two weeks every summer. The divorce made Michael sad and he began to suck his thumb, but he soon got used to the changes and stopped. His mother got married again when he was four years old. He was confused and again felt as if he needed to suck his thumb. He finally felt comfortable with his stepfather and didn't need to suck his thumb any more. His stepfather has a black Labrador dog named Annie.

Michael's mother has no brother, but she has one sister named Amy. Amy is married. Her daughter, Evan, was born when Michael was four years and five months old. Evan is Michael's cousin. Cousin Evan was crying when Michael and his mother visited her and Amy when they came home from the hospital after Evan was born. Michael said, "Evan needs Bunny. I don't need him now. I am a big boy." So, he gave Bunny to Evan. It was the best gift he had to give to her. She rubbed Bunny's ears and quit crying.

When Michael was three years old, Granny got real sick. She had to go to the hospital. She had trouble breathing. The doctor couldn't make her well. The only one who could make her better was Jesus, so she went to live with Jesus at His house.

When Michael went back to visit Granny-Pa, it was lonesome without Granny, but he got used to her not being there. He sometimes wondered when Granny would come home to Granny-Pa's house.

Granny-Pa was a barber. He cut Michael's hair. Granny-Pa liked to tell stories about fishing. He also liked baseball and really liked to watch the St. Louis Cardinals on TV.

Granny-Pa needed friends to be near him. He sold his house and moved into a retirement home. Michael could visit him there. Sometimes Granny-Pa would come to Michael's father's or aunt's home to visit them.

When Michael was five years old, Pa's sister Dorothy, who had been sick a long time, died. Michael went with his mother, Aunt Amy and his baby cousin, Evan, to Aunt Dorothy's funeral in Pocahontas, Arkansas. Michael wondered what a funeral was. His mother told him it would be like a church service. She told him to keep his eyes and ears open and many of his questions would be answered.

The evening before the funeral, the relatives and friends of Aunt Dorothy met at the funeral home for Visitation. Dorothy was his mother's aunt and Michael's great-aunt. Pa and Ma were there and Michael's Aunt Amy and Cousin Evan. Pa's other sisters and their children were also there.

Aunt Dorothy was lying in a casket in a room by herself. A casket is like a box made into a bed on tall legs with wheels. She looked as if she were sleeping. There was a large living room where friends came to visit with the relatives and went in to see Dorothy. Many cried when they looked at her and told her good-bye. The people talked about things that they remembered about Aunt Dorothy and how much they would miss her, but now she wouldn't hurt anymore. There was lots of laughing and crying. Michael didn't know most of the people, but they were glad to see him.

The funeral was held the next day at the funeral home. It was in the chapel, a room like a church.

Aunt Dorothy's casket was at the front, and there were lots of bouquets around and on it. Some bouquets had banners that said, "Mother," "Sister," or "Grandmother." A man sang a song and a minister talked about Aunt Dorothy's life. He told us to remember how she cared about people and liked to laugh. He prayed, read from the Bible, and said we would see her again some day in Heaven.

After the services the people gathered on the front lawn. Michael kept watching the big car in the driveway at the side of the funeral home, without asking questions. Suddenly some men started carrying the casket out to put it into the big car. Michael turned to talk to his mother. She was busy talking to cousins. Michael ran to her, telling her to come quickly, adding, "You are missing the most important part!" He continued watching to know what would happen to Aunt Dorothy.

He later found out the men carrying the casket are called pallbearers and the big car is called a hearse.

All the cars got into a parade line behind the hearse and followed it along the highway to a cemetery far out in the country. Michael, his mother, Aunt Amy, and Evan rode with Pa and Ma in their van. Pa was told to turn his car lights on while driving so other drivers would know he was part of the funeral procession.

At the cemetery there was a tent over a large, deep hole in the ground with a pile of dirt beside it. The pallbearers carried the casket from the hearse to the side of the hole. They put the flowers on the casket and on the pile of dirt. The people gathered around. Ma stayed in the van with Evan, who was asleep. The minister talked awhile and said a prayer. Then the people went to their cars and left. Pa and others took a flower to keep. Pa and his sister, Maudie, walked over to a grave marking where her husband was buried. They also looked at where Pa's mom and dad and two brothers are buried. They all had died.

While they were driving home, Michael said, "Granny died too, didn't she? They put her in the ground, didn't they?"

The next year, when Michael was six, Granny-Pa began to not feel good and needed help with eating and dressing. He moved into a nursing home where there were high beds like in a hospital and nurses to take care of him. Michael could visit him there.

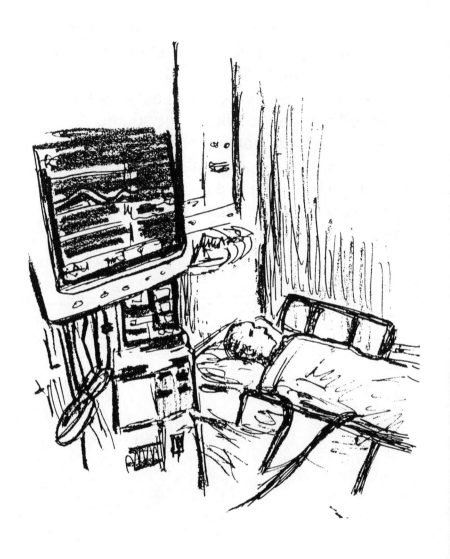

A short while later, Granny-Pa got so sick that he had to go to the hospital. The doctors needed to use machines to help his heart and lungs work better. But they couldn't make him well. He died in the hospital.

Michael went to Granny-Pa's funeral with his father. Ma attended the funeral with Michael's mother. Michael's Uncle Scott told a story about Granny-Pa's life. There was a flag covering Granny-Pa's casket because he was a war veteran. When the casket was taken to the cemetery, the pallbearers took the flag off and folded it. They gave the flag to Michael's father because he was the oldest son. Michael rode home from the funeral with his mother.

While they were driving home, Michael wondered about the many, many grave markers.

Ma said, "Yes, everyone who lives dies at some time. That is part of God's plan."

Michael said, "What if Heaven gets full?"

Ma said, "That won't happen because Jesus is preparing a place for everybody who believes in Him. In God's house, there are many dwelling places." (See John 14:1–3.)

Michael then remembered how Granny-Pa needed someone to care for him in a nursing home. He asked, "Do they have nursing homes in Heaven?"

His mother answered, "No, they don't need them because no one is sick or in pain."

Ma said, "People receive new bodies that aren't crippled and don't hurt." (See Rev. 21:3–45 and 1 Cor. 15:35–44, 49.)

Michael asked, "How do you know?"

Ma said, "That's what the Bible says."

His mother said, "I learned it in Sunday School and I know it is true."

Michael said, "I know you say so, Ma says so, and the Bible says so, but my head doesn't say so."

The next time Michael visited Ma and Pa, Ma got out a Bible story book. In this book was a picture of an old man named John sitting on a rock. He had been put on an island by himself to live and couldn't leave as punishment because he wouldn't quit telling stories about Jesus and the Good News that Jesus is alive, and if we believe Jesus is God's son and follow Him, we too can have eternal life. John wrote the Gospel of John and Revelations, so we can still read his stories.

Michael thought about John and his head began to say that if John was so sure about his stories that he wouldn't stop telling them even after all the punishment he received from other people, what he wrote in the Bible must be true. Michael felt better about his questions, although he knew death and Heaven would always be a mystery of God.

Appendix: Contemporary English Version Holy Bible

John 14:1–3: Jesus said to his disciples, "Don't be worried! Have faith in me. There are many rooms in my Father's house. I wouldn't tell you this, unless it was true. I am going there to prepare a place for each of you. After I have done this, I will come back and take you with me. Then we will be together."

Revelation 21:3–4: I heard a loud voice shout from the throne: "God's home is now with his people. He will live with them, and they will be his own. Yes, God will make his home among his people. He will wipe all tears from their eyes, and there will be no more death, suffering, crying, or pain. These things of the past are gone forever."

1 Corinthians 15:35–44, 49: Some of you have asked, "How will the dead be raised to life? What kind of bodies will they have?" Don't be foolish. A seed must die before it can sprout from the ground. Wheat seeds and all other seeds look different from the sprouts that come up. This is because God gives everything the kind of body he wants it to have. People, animals, birds, and fish are each made of flesh, but none of them are alike. Everything in the heavens has a body, and so does everything on earth. But each one is very different from all the others. The sun isn't like the moon, the moon isn't like the stars, and each star is different.

That's how it will be when our bodies are raised to life. These bodies will die, but the bodies that are raised will live forever. These ugly and weak bodies will become beautiful and strong. As surely as there are physical bodies, there are spiritual bodies. And our physical bodies will be changed into spiritual bodies.

Just as we are like the one who was made out of earth, we will be like the one who came from heaven.